When Gordon asked me to write this foreword I felt proud and honored at first. But then a couple of hours later I started to get a little worried. I am not a talented writer at all and I was scared not being able to find the right words to describe how awesome he is and how touching every single one of his words is.

My words might not be as special and touching as his are, but the day I met Gordon sure is a very special one to me!! It was a work day like no other. I started working at the NoLimitsFitness gym a couple of weeks earlier. I was new to Kamloops and I was still getting used to living on my own so far away from my original home and my family.

While cleaning the gym entrance, I noticed a pair of cowboy boots on the shoe rackets. Curious as I am, I wanted to know who this pair of boots belonged to. I knew from the beginning that the owner of these boots must be someone very unique. Because the gym was very crowded that day, I totally forgot about the cowboy boots until about an hour later - I was just about to empty the dishwasher – I suddenly heard a warm and calming voice. I looked up and saw an older man with greyish hair smiling at me. This man I am talking about was no other than Gordon of course.

He asked me to make two of my favourite smoothie, one for him and one for me. While drinking „Cracker Jaxx" we started talking. The things we talked about in our first conversation were so intimate, meaningful and it felt like we knew eachother for years. There was this bond, this connection between us from the very beginning, which I always thought no one in this world, would ever be able to describe with words. But of course Gord made it possible, as you can see in some of the following poems. In the following weeks and months I always looked forward to seeing Gordon at the gym so we could talk to each other for hours. Gordon made me feel like I was part of his family. He made me feel loved and protected whenever I was around him.

Did you forget about the cowboy boots as I did on the day I met Gord? I am sure you did. To Confess, when Gordon left the gym, I looked down at his feet as he was wearing the same cowboy boots I wondered about earlier.

Dear reader,
In this book you will get the chance to read some of the most beautiful poems somebody has ever written. Gordons words will make you smile, cry and most of all feel things you never felt because of words before. I promise you poems that are pure, touching and honest.
I ask you to appreciate his words, because by publishing them, Gordon reveals his innermost being.
Have fun and enjoy.

Bits n' Pieces Of My Soul

Chapter One

1 Bit's & Pieces

2 That Pretty Face

3 Amazing Curves

4 A Girl Called Whiskey

5 The Machine

6 What She Means to Me

7 Midnight Special

8 No More Flowers

9 Open Your Heart

10 The Pilot

11 Right Amount of Wrong

12 Holy Smoke

13 Those Baby Browns

14 Beautiful Parts

15 Talked To The Stars About You

Bits an' Pieces I've Yet to See

She says I see things in her
that she has never see before
I see, empathy, strength,
and a true desire for one rep more
Yet there are so many bits
and pieces I've yet to see
How does she like her
morning coffee or is it tea
I know she has the
brightest shine in the room
But I don't know how she
deals with a day of gloom
A lover of nature and the trails
that lead to self fulfillment
She looks to a day of hiking
and a Rocky Mountain ascent
Sit before me and hold my hands
while you speak of dreams
Let us walk hand in hand
as we navigate both love and streams
I see her as a gift sent
down from the Gods of Olympus
That have sent her to lead
me as my personal life compass
As I head out on my final days
of this life long quest
I'm impatiently waiting for
that girl to come west

Irreplaceable You

In my years I've but met but one energy like yours
I love the proverbial gust of magic you share
It's not complicated,
the bottom line is simply you care
The energy emanating from your soul is magical
Your hugs actually transcend the touch, the physical
You give freely as if it was your goal, your duty
I wonder, how many neglect to look past
your physical beauty
Thereby failing to see down into your
Wonderfully unguarded soul
Completely missing those bits n' pieces
that make you whole
I'm so fortunate to have been shared
some of your shine
I've taken it in, bottled it up and
drank it like wine

That Pretty Face

Sure going to miss that pretty face
When I pack up and leave this place
Walking in, you give any day a boost
Especially those days when it's needed most
That smile that shines so vivid and bright
Those encouraging words that keep the goal in sight
You are a warrior and proud of muscles you made
Be proud of who you are and the dues you've paid
Although your NFL times have come to and end
I truly hope and believe, I may have found a friend
Should that friend want to share a conversation
Just say the word and I'll snap to attention
Got your back if you're ever in need
Stay safe, stay heathy, Godspeed

Queen of The Court

She takes two steps and a simple

leap towards the net

Her feet shoulder width apart

lands softly with feet set

Bends at the knees and drops into a semi-squat

Eyes the balls trajectory and sets

her sight on the impact spot

Her right arm comes up and

settles back of her shoulder

Arm stretches out and hand forms

somewhat of a cup holder

At that moment she fires all of

her lower body muscles

Drives upwards bringing Quads,

hamstrings, and glutes, into play

Squeezes her core for additional

stabilization, come what may

Now rises above the floor

like she's done it a thousand before

Eyes lock on the dropping ball,

her arm comes forward

with everything she asks it for

Contact as she reaches the apex of her leap

Driving the ball over the net, straight and deep

Fist pump as she knows this is her sport

She is after all, the Queen Of The Court

Amazing Curves

Let me tell you about

some amazing curves

There's the winding hiways

that I love on my bike

There's those soft gentle

curves on a woman I like

I'm going to run a hand down

from her waist to her hip

And feel the softness of her skin
that I find in my grip

Better The End Of Your Biking Days

She says better the end of your
biking days than the end of your days
She be right, she be strong, she be wise
To make use of my time remaining, I'll rise
I'll pick a new hobby of some great concern
Something off the bucket list is what I'll learn
So when I see you next, I'll sing you a song
Summer break, 2021, you'll be back where you belong
You'll walk back through with your eyes wide open
While guarding your heart so it'll never be broken
No reason or concern as there'll be no uninvited
move
Just a couple of friends sitting, enjoying the view
With the summer's long days an' short night
We'll sit by the river under the bright moonlight
The soft sounds of the river's waters flowing along
Quiets the senses while it whispers it's own song
You will be subjected to stories in a poetic storm
I'll witness your bits n' pieces
blending into perfect form
It may take some time but that's ok
cuz we got awhile
I'll talk you into flashing
your biggest beautiful smile
We'll make memories so you don't forget me
When you return back from whence you came
But know I'll never again feel all alone
As I'll carry you in my heart and on my phone

A Woman Called Whiskey

　　　　I want to kiss that
　　　　woman called Whiskey
　　　　I want her to put
　　　　her arms around me
　　　　I'll look deep down
　　　　into her baby blues
　　　　Knowing I could love
　　　　her down to her shoes

The Machine

Take a break, he said as he was concerned
I'll take a break when I'm done and it's earned
The barrel is only half full so I keep on going
It's just bit of lifting, turning,
and some throwing
He said I was working like a bloody machine
When you tell a sixty year old that's real lean
That he's out working you, it seems a little mean
It'll make my smile grow bigger, it would seem
Takes a whole lot of gym hours
With trainers like my twin towers
Coach pushes one more rep with a stern voice
While Kid Chaos sets the main meal choice
Nothing makes a man whose 20 years junior
Look with envy at the older whose physic is leaner
While the younger sips too many chips and beers
The older leaves sweat angels and ignores the years
Toby Keith sings "Don't Let The Old Man In"
While i climb on the bike and take it for a spin
Brothers Osborne is a favourite of mine too
Singing "I Don't Remember Me Before You

What She Means To Me

Freedom is the sound of that fifth gear whine
As I'm pushing down that dotted white line
Got the Harley out and stretching it's legs
Laying it over till I feel it scrapping the pegs
Technically I'm alone with this bike in flight
But she's always with me when I ride or write
She's that special one that just fits real well
Our souls meld together it was so easy to gel
She guides me and my bike thru the curves
And thinking of her always settles my nerves
She's here when I sit at my desk and hold a pen
Her shine pushes thru the darkness once again
She has the most amazing shine I've ever seen
Spending time with her is living the dream
I'll tell her about the beauty that I see
What she brings, and what she means to me

Midnight Special

Like the Midnight Special
she shines all over me
Her strut shows her confidence
is back, so we see
She radiates and sends out
positive vibes all around
Stands tall and proud while
straightening her crown

No More Flowers

You realize, saying no more flowers
Is akin to stealing superman's powers
Or pulling the mask off the Lone Ranger
It's simply fraught with stranger danger
You know you'll have your down days
If can't send daisies, I'll need other ways
Maybe a cab delivery of a certain kinda tea
An XL, two chia bags, and a half of honey
Dead people get flowers and you're still alive
How do I solve the conundrum, when I arrive
I got it - Oh yes I believe I do!!!
A poem about flowers is what I'll spew
So here it is. On top of the roses
Sat the daisies in special poses
Wrapped around an XL coffee with two milk
Careful now so you don't spill on that gown of silk
Try as she might she sees flowers in her mind
Knowing that tricky bastard got her this time
Her shine bounces back as she's all aglow
Happy he hung around cuz he's good to know

Open Your Heart

Will you please open your heart
and let me love you
Instead of putting up walls
for me to push through
You stood there with
something on your mind
Unwilling to share your
thoughts that may be unkind
Or is it perhaps that they'll
hurt you more than me
Using words like faking and with
you having a solid plan B
There you go talking down
to me but settling for content
Looking over your shoulder
wondering where happiness went
That's when you'll miss me
and our convos the most
You'll be sipping screwdrivers
and talking to a ghost
Where you going to be when
the other boot hits the floor
Tattered and torn knowing
what's likely to be in store

The Pilot

There's a pretty girl that walks in the woods,
to lose her mind and to feed her soul
She wanders along the board walk
on the edge of the lake feeling whole
Had some heath issues and a wee little scare
but hitched up her pants and off to play ball
She knows that fear is a big fat liar
So she focuses on the fact she'll soon be a flyer
Was time to seek changes and redemption
To step back from her previous life of consumption
This new life requires a look inward to her self
Taking better care of her mind and her health
She got folks who love her and got her six
We love n' respect her and not in it for kicks
We look to the days she takes us for a flight
Doing a barrel roll would be a hell of a sight
Imagining the days she flys a float plane
Cruising her island from her airborne reign

Right Amount Of Wrong

McCraw - I need a shot of whiskey
and to smoke that cigarette
I've broken free of those addictions
and stay as far away as I can get
I wanna ride across beautiful
province of British Columbia
The desire so strong it's driving me
Crazy like a bad case of insomnia

Holy Smoke

They called her Holy Smoke
on the street
She was street wise, never accepted defeat
With family she was the
ultimate polite young lady
But the streets pulled her
into a life that's real shady
She was an abused child
when she came into foster care
At thirteen, already a chip on
her shoulder she'd openly wear
She'd hitchhike up highway
sixteen every other Friday
And I'd lecture her upon her
return every other Sunday
Stayed with us for a total
of six intriguing months
Then left to return to
her family and home for once
She was a good foster child
but had some painful issues
And when she was angry she'd
empty a whole box of tissues
Said no one was to love her,
no one was to care
She was stuck in the system
and that's why she's there
Called after two years gone,
asked if we still did the foster thing
Said she had someone who
needed the help we could bring
The one regret is that I never
followed up on that caller
We will all remember her as a
fighter, a scrapper, and a brawler
Her mug shot is a dull black and grey
showing her lifeless eyes and her suffer
Oh but she had such a beautiful
heart and soul!!
You should have seen her in color

Those Baby Browns

You showed up on match one morn
That Duchenne smile and those baby browns
Somewhere Van Morrison is singing about you
I can tell that you're about to make a mistake
I can see your lower lip begin to quiver and shake
One shot at this thing called life
I've always known something was missing
From the top of your crown
Down to where your toes touch the ground
So calm so cool
Being right here in paradise- twice
I hear the sound that scrapping pegs make
A voice in my head says Ride safely for Christ sake

Beautiful Parts

The most
beautiful
parts of her
are the
ones you
cannot see.
They are
her dreams,
her wishes,
her goals,
and her desire
to be the best
she can be

Talked To The Stars About You

She says "I talked to the stars about you'
They replied that he can find a friend in you
She's talks often to both the stars and the moon
Listen carefully you'll hear her whispers it a tune
She speaks of the love that has found a home
A heart vacant for so long, it doesn't need to roam
He makes her shine so much brighter these days
Is it his touch, his voice, or his troubadour ways
A fixer of things and someone to massage her scars
Reminds her, that the great things can't be found in bars
His years are lacking but he an old soul at heart
Wisdom displayed as he puts the horse before the cart
One thing at a time, take time to do it right and not on a whim
Remind him constantly of what you see as the best in him
It may be time to hit that button that will generate posts
But on the upside it'll push away the fakers and the ghosts
Happiness is a fleeting beast and to be handled with care
Feed it generously at every chance or it'll return to it's lair
Look into your heart, take a risk and ride that fucking train
You have weathered the thunder storms, now dance in the rain.

Chapter Two

16 Into Your Very Soul

17 Blank Canvas

18 A Simple Touch Of Your Skin

19 Stole The Light From Your Eyes

20 Sound Of Your Voice

21 Continent Away

22 That Same Warm Feeling

23 She Smiles Real Big

24 Dreamer Without A Dreamer

25 Never Apologize

26 Some Many Things To Say

27 A Splash Of Yellow Amongst The Green

30 Two To Go

31 Forever Friend

32 Where And When

33 If I Could Read Your Mind

34 Oktoberfest 2022

35 Best Days Of Your Life

36 Your Word

37 When She Walks In

38 No Place To Go

39 Appetite For Success

40 Magical Mystical You

Into Your Very Soul

I see your instagram pic looking out at me
Beautiful brown eyes reaching out a plea
I can feel them showing me a fabulous goal
As I fall in and swim deep down into your very soul
Your soul wraps around me like a soft velvet glove
A feel so beautifully strange, but it's a feeling of love
I can feel your heart beat synchronize with mine
Two hearts blending and merge into a single life line
Soulmates bound forever and for all eternity
For all future generations, for us and posterity
I'll be with you, when we stand on that Pacific beach
While we stare at the stars that are just out of reach
I'll be in your heart, your thoughts, and your mind
I'll be with you "no matter what'
as you're truly, one of a kind

Blank Canvas

He says
he wears
black so
people
have a
blank
canvas on
which to
tell their
tales of
things
they
know
nothing
of.

A Simple Touch of Your Skin

Ok so now where would you like to begin
I'm thinking with a simple touch of your skin
As you know, as soon as I saw you, I knew
There was an amazing soul deep inside you
I'll hang around on the edge of that line
I'll do whatever it takes to make you mine
I'll love you for the amazing creature you are
My goal is simply to love you from near and far
To pick you up when you fall to your knees
And I'll help you heal your scars with ease
An inquiring mind will find the softness of your being
Gently exploring your thoughts with a goal and a meaning
To seek out those few things that bring you woe
To tackle them one by one and make them leave and go
I think, my beautiful friend that I compliment
We are to embark on an adventure of confident
Show you the trust and faithfulness that you need
To halt the madness and those feeling will recede

Stole The Light From Your Eyes

Who or what was it that stole that light from your eyes
I know the coroner said it was those damn cocaine highs
Your meds couldn't do what you wanted them to do
So you went to the street and were dead before you knew
That damn depression that was relentless and kept calling
Pulling you into the shadows and your skin to crawling
No amount of rest or sleep would satisfy him and send it away
The darkness was all encompassing and wasted another day
I cry as I was never there to hold your hand
Too ignorant to even acknowledge that depression existed
Warned you what those cigarettes would do to your heart
Asked you numerous times to quit and to never again start
However the depression, anxiety, the meds were too much to bear
So street meds were your goto state and they don't really care
I'm sure they chase the depression away from you short term
But they stole your smile and the light from your eyes long term

The Sound of Your Voice

I miss the sound of your spoken word
A unique sound sweeter than any I've heard
I love the softness of your whispered voice
When you share thoughts with me by choice
Which is it I miss, the words or the sound?
I miss them both when you're not around
We spoke of wishes and of dreams
Of hikes, and running, and different teams
I wonder when I will whisper into your ear
Some of these poems that you find so dear
You find a spot on that river bank for two
I'll sit beside an relay poems of missing you
Just remember that I love you and that I care
No matter where you are I'll always be here
You're welcome to lean on me for support
You'll find me front of line waiting at the airport

Continent Away

Worried a continent away
for her well being
Come tears of pearl to guard
her against the unseeing
However I'll wait
those many weeks
When I hug her there'll
be emotional peaks
And hug her I will too
Tight to my chest
feeling truly blessed

That Same Warm Feeling

I'll get that same warm feeling
of a shot of whisky going down
When I ride in on my bike
into your heart and into your town
As the morning sunbeams break
I'll take all the love you offer and make
Looking to feel that curve of your hips
and the taste of whiskey on your lips
When I get that first long slow kiss
I'll cherish moments with you like this

She Smiles Real Big

She smiles real big, gives her butt a little pat
Said this would look really great, sitting on that
She wears that blue bandana with real country pride
Looks real good sitting up on that big blue ride
I'm thinking there's no way
I'm gonna leave, you see
Until she hangs out, with an outlaw like me
She throws a leg over that bike
and smiles real wide
Wraps her arms around my waist an' tickles my side
Her big blue eyes match her long blond hair
Feeling her against my back gives me reason to care

Dreamer Without A Dream

What's a dreamer without a dream
What's an angel without her wings
It's about the dreams never realized
Or those moments I was compromised
She's got a wild whiskey heart
Been known to tear a bar apart
Along with a sweet gentle soul
On a good day she rains love whole
Occasionally allows me to tag along
Careful I am, so as to not get this wrong

Never Apologize

Takes 5 as the virus
shuts training down
All of her schooling,
and all of her town
She finds home workouts
are the best
With her pup on her
back taking a rest
She will come out of
this better than most
As she has no quit in her,
nor does she boast
She opened something in me
causing words to flow
Her hugs are so full of love
they actually glow
I tell her to never apologize
for having the brightest shine
Be proud, you as a highly sensitive
one, are so very fine
Be safe and take care and
embellish the world's providing
Me? I'm good and it's warm
outside so I'm going riding

So Many Things To Say

It's about the girl with the sad eyes and wet hair
I know there's an untold story, so tell me with care
But the story I want to hear is the one
behind those eyes
I've seen that look before and it
reminds me of goodbyes
Those eyes carry some kindness
but also some despair
Maybe thinking about someone to hold,
someone to care
So tell us the story of your life, and make if kind
We'll take some happiness wherever it we can find
She has many things to say but
cannot find the words
Time's are tough when a wordsmith
has lost her verbs
Or is it her voice that gives up
and begins to quiver
As we know that a special kiss
can make her skin shiver
A diamond is just pressure applied
to a lump of coal
So I can begin to imagine
what she hides in her soul
When she release those bonds we'll see her shine
It'll be wondrous, joyous, and definitely by design
So speak those words and let loose your tales
We listen impatiently to hear of roads and trails
The road you walk has been travelled by very few
To get to where you need to be, just keep being you

A Slash of Yellow Amongst The Green

Driving along we see that singular yellow tree amongst all the green
We wonder and ask why it shines like the jewels of a righteous queen
It' shines like the solitary stone in the ring of the bride and lover
With a stray beam catching and refactoring into an array of colour
To many it looks like the demarcation between order and chaos
Or that one in a million bet you laid down in LasVegas
I know a woman that is like that splash of yellow a blanket of green
She is an anomaly as she just isn't the norm nor is she the same
She fears not of controversy and ignites excited conversation
By posting subjects like dating, sports, and participation
She dreams of walking with the wolves and feeling their freedom
And despises those sorry souls that commit treason
She says we're on this earth to see each other through
Such is an example of her wondrous heart and soul
She shines every bit as bright as a morning sunrise
And like Venus she outshines everyone else in the skies
Singular in her love of her team and affection is never spared
A happy bunch for they are hugged, and lovingly shared.
She trains them on her own and showers them with her shine
They have no choice but to absorb it, as Jesus' disciples did with wine

Two To Go

First year successfully complete
and only two more to go
Take a wee break, rest for a wee bit
then once again hit the show
You can tell her mood by the way
she moves and by her strut
With her work ethics and training
she knows she made the cut
Test may have stressed her out
but now she's good to go
Her heart and soul has no quit in them,
we know that's so

Forever Friend

She be strong and she be fearless
She's a positive thinker and hard to impress
Has a gorgeous smile to complete a beautiful face
Impressive as she puts every workout in it's place
Her IG account gives me reason to laugh and smile
Especially considering I haven't done it in a while
That smile of her's shining so vivid and bright
And her words that help to keep the goal in site
When she wishes to swap stories of words
We'll sit quietly in Starbucks like a couple on nerds
Although her Canadian days have come to an end
I know that I have made a forever friend

Where And When?

Where and when do I get to see you next
There's not enough of you in a little bitty text
October 22 I'll be there to see you rise
Photographing you beneath your flag is the prize
To witness you fulfill your biggest dream
I'll be so full of pride, I'll surely bust a seam
I'm so proud of you and the goals you achieve
You are unstoppable as long as you believe
Believing in you is an honour and no stretch
Your Canadian family's pride is difficult to match
We are happy to call you one of our own
And send you to Europe on a friendly loan
We expect you to return when the world gets right
We will meet you at the smoothie bar at 1st light
We'll toast to the woman you've become
Where you go, where you are, and where you're from

If I Could Read Your Mind

If I could read your mind, what does it hold
What secrets are wanting out? Wanting to be told
No! No, your secrets are yours to keep
Knowing them may cause me to cry or weep
What stories would it be willing to tell
Could I find the answer to your magical spell
I'd find that you believe in somethings
Along with the kind of things that love brings
What thoughts make your knees weak
Is it that forehead kiss or one on your cheek
I wonder? Would I find the last time you felt alone?
Or the painful memory when you broke that bone
I'll look to your happiest thoughts for guidance
To take you where you find solitude, your silence
I'd find the scent of your favourite perfume
And how it lifts you out, of that feeling of doom
It tells me of your coffee with plenty of milk
As well as your wish for scarfs of silk
Looking deep, I see strong self confidence
That hails from experience and consequence
At last my ego wishes to know, do you love me so
Thank you for sharing thoughts and dreams
Give me your best as I'm yours forever it seems
Like bees returning to their honeycomb
It's time for you to come on home

Oktoberfest 2022

As I'm not much of a party guy or drinker
More of a wallflower, loner, and a thinker
However there's going to be a celebration
During Octoberfest in a faraway nation
I'll definitely be attending this event
For a special woman who has 3 long years, spent
When I touch down, I'll simply seek the brightest shine
For she outshines all city lights, a most beautiful sign
She'll be standing proud of who she has become
Strong, intelligent, great personality and then some
Very few in my 64 years, have made such an impression
She outworks everyone during each and every session
Meeting her is one of the best things ever happened to me
She makes me homesick for places I've yet to see
Hopefully she guides us to see more than beer steins
Perhaps A fourteen century castles' remains
There be one special site above all else that I wish to visit
Her beautiful smile along with the warmth of her hug given

Best Days Of Your Life

These are the best days of your life
Heading in whatever direction you like
As you become the woman
you are meant to be
On track to achieve your goals,
focus is the key
It's 3 in the morning
as I listen to the rain
Such a soothing sound
to my overworked brain
Your shine dazzles all
with its brilliance
As you begin your day
without reluctance
There will come a day when
a thousand voices will call your name
Because as a leader of men and woman
you've stepped up your game

Your Word

Your word
is your
bond
Guard it
carefully
as it is the
only thing
you truly
own
If you see
a wrong,
fix it your self

When She Walks In

It's six thirty when she walks in the front door
No sign of the previous days workout or being sore
Familiar with a few of the regulars she forms a smile
And nods to several folks as she walks down the aisle
She's a brown eyed brunette wears her hair in a bun
She has work ethic that's amazing and second to none
Dumbbells on the bench start the day
Proud, determinedand does it her way
She sets up, pulls twenty's off the dumbbell rack
Decline sit-ups tightenher core n' six pack
It may be her sculptured body that draws eyes
However it's her no quit attitude that's the real prize
Appears she just makes it up as she goes
No coach, no book, It's like she just knows

No Place To Go

They say grief is love with no place to go
I believe it to be true and that it's so
It hurts when you lose a loved one
Can't help feeling down and done
I've cared and loved twenty-nine years
When on July 17 that energy disappears'
Try as I might the tears no longer fall
As I refuse to believe why his Lord did call
But I look for the beauty in the broken
Always thankful for last words spoken
Love you is always the last word heard
Love you too Dad, was the parting word
Collateral beauty is hard to find at times
Writing words helps as I add more lines
I feel his energy flow through when I write
As i now leave a legacy to follow that light
Kyle - watch over your sister and brother
Nieces, nephews as well as friends and other.
                       Love you always, Dad

Appetite for Success

How strong is your appetite for success
Is your work ethic your home address
Do you push through every challenge
Have you dumped all your baggage
Your dreams are real and true
Find that truth that drives thru
Drives your pursuit of excellence
Hammers through with persistence
Train with your mind on task
So you react without the mask
Reactions should be automatic
Lack of response could be tragic
Let your workout be your voice
You've taken this route by choice
For those that lead there's life out there
Breaking trails while treading with care

Magical, Mystical You

Beneath your physical beauty
Is the magical, mystical you
Though you shine brighter by the day
I'm still going to check that you're ok
Now I know your dreams will come true
Regardless of the pain you've been through
Because I seen that faraway look in your eye
Knowing those recent pains have healed and said
goodbye
You're like a spring sunrise
following the darkest night
I see new life in your soul filling you with light
As you pass the mirror you will see
your reflection shine
Maybe it's something you haven't noticed
in a long time
It's there with refreshed confidence
Taking on life with regained opulence
Call it renewed, refreshed and now rebuilt
Your crown no longer sits with that sad little tilt
So you are no longer burdened with that pain
As a resilient woman,
you're feeling truly alive again
Now give me one of those hugs that speak to my soul
The ones that put starlight in my eyes and make me
whole

Chapter Three

41 Never Needed My Given Name

42 Mustang Girl

43 Highway 12 Wreck

44 Turn Loose That Rebel Yell

45 Guard Your Shine

46 She Knows

47 Strong Enough

48 Virus Of 2020

49 Smile At A Stranger

50 Your Shine Is Easy To Love

51 Peace By Piece

52 Tired Of Walking This Road Alone

53 Forehead Kisses

54 Nowhere Special

55 Whatever You Need Me To Be

56 Good For My Soul

57 171,476 Words

58 My Own Hevenly Way

59 Single Chat

60 Coming Home

61 Brown Eyed Girl

62 If This Bike Could Talk

63 The Story I'd Like To Hear

64 To Be A Cop

65 What Whiskey Does

Never Needed My Given Name

The best times of my life
I never needed my given name
But the titles given me,
were priceless just the same
Dad, son, brother,
popa, and father
There's always a favourite,
like none other!
When she whispers
to my very soul, Hey Hon
As I know she's now looking for fun
But the best of them all
is when you hear Thks Babe
I needed those words to get me
They say that pleasure
is the absence of pain
Take me as I'm ready
Go slow but go steady j

Mustang Girl

She's one of those girls
Doesn't need diamonds and pearls
Rather strap on a Mustang five speed
Big tires, an' noisy pipes y'all best heed
Goes zero to sixty in nothing flat
Hair tied up, kinda like it like that
Blue bandana tied in back
As she heads for the track

Highway 12 Wreck

Sun breaks on a hot August morn great for chasing white line stripes
Perfect day to take Gypsy out and sounding off it's pipes
I'll take #1 to Cache Creek listening to that fifth gear whine
Then take a left onto 97 and 15 kilometres north to ninety nine
From the turnoff to Lillooet is a favourite to scrape the pegs
My bike glides thru those twisties while stretching it's legs
Pass by the Graymont Lime Plant like a ghost
Couple miles then Turquoise Lake plays host
Crown Lake gives way to Marble Canyon Provincial Park
Pavilion Lake community's drop in speed causes pipes to bark
The last two mles lakeside we dodge rocks on the road
Now into cattle country and a whole new episode
Nothing left of the Pavilion General but a stone chimney
Standing tall and alone like the last guard standing sentry
Eyes wide open now as the sheep are out and about
It's a clear ride until the fountain tunnel work area appears
Drop down to 2nd gear, giving a nod to the flagman
Cross the slide area without missing a beat
Crossed Fountain Flats then looking up the Bridge River valley
Dropped down and crossed the Bridge of Camels to the finale
Top of the Station Hill is my destination of this spin
Lillooet Graveyard holds a good number of my kin
Most missed is my mother and mentor, Doreen Rose
Chatted to her a bit about Kyle & the life I chose
Into town, gas up and something to quench my thirst

Hottest town in BC that day with the sun at it's worst
No sense riding back on 99 when there's hiway twelve waiting
So turned east and got those tires to spinning and rotating
Pulled over and had a snack and a sip of water
Tried to recall if I had sent a text to my daughter
A V-Rod blew by me like he was on a mission
Wasn't about to chase him down as I'm unfamiliar with road condition
Into gear, onto the pavement, ran up the gears
Hiway speed was enough to feel the wind and my eyes to tear
Uneventful for thirty K or so then hell broke loose
Entered a right hander at normal highway speed
Seen a 3/4 curl Ram on the side having a feed
He stepped onto the pavement and settled broadside
Over the center line but I couldn't clear him in stride
Over reacted and hard down on the rear brake
Locked up the rear and held it straight with everything I could take
Thirty or more then it began to slide and knew i was going down
Sideways for a wee bit then something found solid
Ejected over the bars, both body and bike airborne
Hit the pavement, arms wishing leathers I'd worn
Broke my right arm while negotiating that landing and the fall
My parkour training kicked in and did one shoulder roll I recall
Took a bump on the helmet and lost a bit of skin
But lived through it so there will be no gathering of the kin
Bike is in the shop and will be repaired and I will ride again
I may ride a little slower, and riding again doesn't mean Im insane
I thank God and Coach for making me grittier than the rest
Been asked if I'll quit riding but nope I've yet to ride my best

Turn Loose That Rebel Yell

Don't be afraid to turn loose that rebel
in you every once in a while
Pull on your big girl boots
and strut your style
Use those boots to kick holes in the
darkness till your shine bleeds through
The world ain't yours yet,
try as you might, to your eat be true
Go ahead and take your shot
Give it your best try, claim your spot
Shine so bright your friends gotta wear shades
Glasses so dark, folks start playing charades
They know not how to handle your dazzle
To them you're are a riddle, or a puzzle
Always the weird one that never groveled
Always inclined to take the road less travelled
Lay down some tracks for others to follow
Cuz following others is hard for you to swallow

Guard Your Shine

Monday morn I had the strangest feeling
as I scrolled on thru
Cuz I could see the shine coming off
those beautiful two
Eyes that allow us to see down into
their unguarded soul
Cheerful and happy cuz that's
just how they roll
What does it take to daily
maintain that beautiful view
To shake the cobwebs and sleep
as they're an early crew
Smiling is required to all that
use this selfie state
They're here to take on the world
with a clean slate
One thing I will suggest to you two,
time after time.
Guard it carefully and don't let anyone,
Steal Your Shine

She Knows

Sometimes what you do comes on too strong
Sometimes what you say comes out wrong
No need to impress the girl as she already knows
She sees past your little bullshit shows
Compassion is her weapon of choice
She feels more than she'll ever say
People shy away as they don't understand
How she knows things she's never been taught
Deals in things mystical and magical
Cognizant to worldly events that are tragical
I too, know of thoughts before they're spoken
Nods from associates that are obviously token

Strong Enough

Don't know why I thought you
were nothing short of perfection
Or was it, just a feeling
that you loved attention
Self confidence is a
stranger, far too often
Many a time it
makes my heart soften
Lately, you, like the days,
have grown stronger
Life's lessons have taken hold,
your story speaks with honour
Seen a post that spoke to me
Which said that I was to
share it with thee
Said your heart had scars from
spending time with toxicity
It kept fighting, beating and believing
Causing you to open your arms
to the world whispering
I still love you as I am strong enough

The COVID-19 Virus of 2020

Those amazing folks in blue and green
The strongest people we've seen ivj
They step between the virus and me
While we watch the TSE dive into the sea
Ships afloat with no place to run
Planes loaded with sick people come
Assisted living folks hit hard,
and again stand sentry
That's the thanks they get,
for building this country?
Six feet is a life time away from grandkids
As the regulators and rulers now forbids
Stress turns good folks bad, bitching begins
No one willing to forgive another man's sins
Prison guards unappreciated and nervous
But hang in there, doing their job an' service
Bylaw officers are treated poorly and shunned
Canals and river clean up an' folks are stunned
Stay safe has been a biker salute for many years
Today it's used by all,
with their eyes full of tears
How do we thank all those unknown employees
Normally forgotten but now our hero's are these
The restauranteurs doing take out and curb side
The seamstress' making masks sewn and tied
Canadian pride circle hospitals at precisely seven
God sent these healers straight from heaven
So count your blessings, set down, and read a book
You'll find that you stayed safe for all the time
it took

Smile at a Stranger

Smile at a stranger and see what happens
It's no surprise that she gets a few tap ins
That gentle smile boosts the soul off the chart
She has kindest of soul and the warmest of heart
For fun she trains her herd of two
Followed around by two dogs of blue
She's a true lover of all four legged critters
Although that Hank horse has the jitters
Now let's get back to that Duchenne smile
That she flashes every once in a while
First I seen it I was an unknown
But now she treats me as one of her own
She says she has a bit of a interesting past
Hard to believe as she'll now
do anything she's asked
I'm happy to back her in whatever she do
And I'm fortunate to be
included as one of her crew

Your Shine Is Easy To Love

Your shine is easy to love
Show me the dark side
I'll begin to love you even more
There's a whisper on the street
The waiting is unbearable and unending
Drop your walls and show me your scars
Bullet riddled heart and wounded soul
I'll do my best to you remind you who I am
Remember that I'm a fan of yours
I've long been under your magical spell
just when I begin to think I know you
You disappear into the eastern skies
My only wish is to walk by your side
To smile, to be happy, to know you're safe
To know that I'm here for you

Peace by Piece

Peace by piece is her business name
Appropriate as finding peace is her game
Professionally trained to help us heal and cope
She teaches us to stay away
from that slippery slope
She deals in depression, anxiety, and grief
Gently spoken words designed to bring relief
Will make a few targeted inquirries about the past
Knows first hand that some pains are wide and vast
Only took one session and she made
the Bring a Book Club
She's inspirational and
knows which scar to give a rub
Soft spoken and carries a
pain only a mother knows
The lose of a child is pain
that never leaves, never goes
She not only lost a son, but a husband too
I wish the world would do, what i want it to
Says grief is love with no place to go
I believe that's true, I believe it's so
I, like many others, look to her for guidance
I appreciate her listening
as well as her indulgence
We talked of time and it's limited amount
As well as how we are to pay that account
Although this kind of pain
will crush you if you let it
You just can't take the pain out of the hurt
Because we are made of magic and resilience
We are to look to great memories
and their brilliance
Like a runaway train brought under control
This woman's energy is pure gold and warms the soul

Tired of Walking This Road Alone

Tired of walking this road all alone
There's days it hits right to the bone
I see you bring forth your brightest shine
So proud that I can call you a friend of mine
But you're so many many miles away
I want someone to talk to on this day
You always lifted me up when i felt down
Now at the gym there's no-one like you around
Every day I think of your infectious smile
As well as those hugs that last a good while
I am reminded of your physical beauty
Is it rude to mention your cute shapely booty
I read the story about hustle over luck
Bring it hard! Like getting hit by a truck
I look to the day you return, your hair in a mess
Hug you close with your head on my chest
Looking so beautiful without any make up on
Like a spring morning sun breaking the dawn
You may not have intended to change my life
Check with your heart, You'll find I meant no strife
So I take this opportunity to ask forgiveness
As my intention was for love and kindness

Forehead Kisses

A kiss unlike any others
Never lustful, never smothers
A kiss that is so powerful
Nothing else is so wonderful
A kiss on the cheek shows friendship
It occurs often to reduce tension
To comfort when feeling lost or down
As well to fix the tilt in her crown
A kiss on the lips is full of lust
After you establish significant trust
It starts you on a physical journey
Watch where it takes you in a hurry
Something about a forehead kiss
That stands out something like this
Kinda like old time rock and roll
It goes right down into the soul
It builds an emotional connection
Along with an intelligent affection
It says I love you, not for your body
But for you just being you, for me
This kiss it about love and respect
Showing that desire to simply connect
Says I got your back like you have mine
So when I see you next, just wait in line
For I will give you a true forehead kiss
Sending unbridled friendship like this
Your soul will fill with warmth and glow
As off on an adventure you will undoubtable go

No Where Special

Where would you like to go so we can sit and talk
He follows her down the path and onto the dock
No where special she says with a enormous smile
Someplace quiet, where we can be alone for awhile
Off come the boots and dips her feet in the water
So warm she says, hope it don't get any hotter
My big old Harley that will take you for a ride
Strap on that bike, wrap your legs round each side
We'll leave this town running and gunning
He's a handsome dude and she be stunning
Onto this new adventure they've just begun
Both leaving behind, naughty things they done
She stole a diamond ring from a real bad man
And he cut and ran from a fight with the clan
High tailing down that long dotted white line
Looking for the magical place to stop and dine
They pull into the roadside diner, look at the sign
No shirts, no shoes, no service, no time to shine
No guns, no knives, and best be real careful
As you've stopped at the diner at No Where Special

Whatever You Need Me To Be

She says she can't love me
the way that I want
I'm know she's serious
and not there to flaunt
I want to be the ears
that listen to your woe
To be the shoulder you
lean on wherever you go
To be the voice in your head
that speaks of your beauty
Be the speaker of your shine,
as that's my pleasure, my duty
I want to be there on any
of those dark and lonely days
As well as on the good times
and during your glory phase
I know of your fondness of
conversations and for healthy food
I'll do whatever it takes to raise
a smile and lift your mood
You're safe with me so trust me
with your heart, mind, and soul
You'll not be disappointed as
I'll pay whatever is the toll
So please bear with me while
we're on this trail
As I'm good with my word
and I will not fail
I'll look into your eyes and
tell you flat out you see
That I know what I want!
It's whatever you need me to be.

Good For My Soul

In her daily life
she can't help but care
It's her nature to
be kind and to share
She'll step up when
most turn an' walk away
When trouble walks in
she alone will stand and stay
To hold the hand of
a lost soul or stranger
I fear for her as she puts
herself in front of danger
When she hugs you it's like medicine
I'm so grateful to have her in my life
as she is definitely good for my soul

If I Could See The Future

What if I could see the future
My past has seen many a suture
I look to better times
I write to better rhymes
I'll put words together
That they may last forever
Although My heart belongs to you
This nightmare is mine to live through
Will I be weak or will I be strong
Will I be right or will I be wrong
The future belongs to me
Just need to find the key
Is it country or rock and roll
That saves my soul
Don't know why I'm still alive
Tired of the alone life jive
Time to go biking
As it's to my liking
Going forward yard by yard
Looking to play my last card
There will come a day to confess
I badly need a change of address

171,476 Words

171,476 words in the english language
As I sit here dumbfounded in anquish
Try to find words that are true and fit
It's a difficult chore I must admit
She's pulchritudinous and aesthetic
Passionate, ambitious, and athletic
Cordial, popular and gregarious
with a massive smile that's contagious
Her empathy encourages her to be generous
She's exuberant, ebullient, and adventurous
Not to mention, scintillating, and ingenuity
Intelligence in abundance, as is her curiosity
I absolutely admire and cherish that shine
Respected and appreciated like strawberry wine
She will forever be carried in my mind and soul
Call it love, infatuation,
irrespective I'll gladly pay toll
I can take all of the above and
with today's technology
Replace 171,476 words,
with this one little emoji
♡

My Own Heavenly Way

It's been a long and hard road
with the odd calamity.
To build my circle of friends and build a family
To ensue I wake up with nothing but love
and peace in my heart and soul
I know you understand that my love
of you is unconditional and the goal
It's to be as strong tomorrow as it was yesterdays
That famous smile of yours compares
to the one Mona Lisa conveys
Her smile is nowhere near as contagious
Nor her heart as strong, driven, and courageous.
You are in my life till my last day
Even then I'll keep in touch in my own heavenly
way.

Single Chat

It may have been just a single chat
across the smoothie bar counter
Many more were sure to follow
that first amazing encounter
However Celine, that conversation
meant the world to me.
Your kindness, and your beautiful soul
were so obvious to see
You followed that with but
one of your amazing hugs so fine
Like those of a child there was
no resistance nor any sign
Many more chats were to
come in the months that pass
Preceding each of those chats,
a hug with just a wee bit of sass
Like those of a child there
was no resistance nor any sign
Many more chats were to come
in the months to follow
Each preceding those chats,
a hug as if straight from Apollo

Coming Home

Regardless of where you live or roam
When you are with me you are 'home'
No need for costumes or building a wall
As I'll come running whenever you call
Home is where you will always feel secure
You'll feel loved, safe, with a soul so pure
Free to take your time, and your solitude
To rest and recharge your soul, your mood
Home will be that spot on my left chest
Where your head will rest at it's best
My heart beat will synchronize with your veins
As my soul absorbs your griefs and your pains
Believe in me loving you the way you love
Like a warm and gentle hand from above
Giving everything is the way it was meant
This is what it means, to give,
at a hundred percent
You are my thoughts as I close my eyes
And for this night I say my goodbyes
While in my nights dreams, you'll roam,
You will always be, coming home!

If This Bike Could Talk

The stories this bike could tell
It would speak of long lonely roads
I'll speak of pulling over
to call that girl in my thoughts
Pull over as that pretty girl is in my head
As I sit, I dismount and drop to a knee
I've just seen a post about a biker going down
She's with me cruising up along the lakes
And as I follow the route Simon Fraser makes
Across the Rockies down thru Roger's Pass
Now highways will fall away real fast

The Story I'd Like To Hear

The story I'd like to hear
is the one behind those eyes
I've seen that look before,
it reminds me of goodbyes
Those eyes carry kindness and
promises of something to share
Looking for someone to hold,
as well as someone to care!
And care I do when selfies I see
and feel with what they do to me
I sit down, then send once a week,
my heartfelt written words to speak
So take these hands that write
these words of love and delight
Treat them as gentle and kind
as you would treat my mind.
They wish to hold you best
with your head on my chest

To Be A Cop eh?

To make your mark on this earth
To show the world your worth
Your workouts have to be on task
Your eyes burn till you don the mask
You will join the forces of urgency
Injecting certainly into uncertainly
Calming the storm will be your norm
Be first to stand and to show your brand
You will show that officer in the mirror
There childhood dream became clear
Never to give up, nor to turn tail
To offer a hand to the hurt and to the frail
Disrespected through no fault of your own
Hold your anger and stay in your zone
Keep those people that are under your care
Safe and sound while they speak to prayer
There will be days when you feel lost
You'll will win your place, you'll pay the cost
Respect the opposition, so you they don't surprise
Show them kindness, compassion as their prize
Every event will have it's collateral beauty
Look for it, seek it out as that is your duty

What Whiskey Does

Randy Houser sings he's gonna let
whiskey do what whiskey does
I'm looking forward to feeling what
whiskey does an' when I feel that buzz
She's the kinda girl that'll dance on the bar
And looks right at home in that vintage car
I think she'll feel real good holding my hand
When we spend the day walking this land
An Alberta girl that fortunately landed in BC
I'll be a happy man when she walks with me

Chapter Four

66 I've Got Your Back

67 Catch Her If You Can

68 God Spent More Time On You

69 A Girl Like Mine

70 Miss That Face

71 We Will Meet Again

72 Minutes

73 Bit's An Pieces

74 She Makes Me Feel

75 Nothing But A Dream

76 Yoho Mountains

77 Far From Where She Started

78 Stuck In My Head

79 Over Qualified

80 Fire In Her Eyes

81 Be That Girl

82 Dancing In The Moonlight

83 Glass Castles

84 The Scent Of Water

85 Thoughts Put To Pen

86 Hair is Bloodshot Red

I've Got Your Back

I've got your back or I've got your six
What does it mean, when you're in a fix?
It means I'll step between you and your trouble
I'll pick you up and hold you when you struggle
We all go through some down times and hard times
And occasionally we need redemption for our crimes
When the haters start on your life and your living
I'll defend you all the while
for being so kind and giving
So on this upcoming birthday
when we all hold you dear
I need to speak of the beauty
you see in your mirror
The confidence is growing stronger,
the shine grows brighter
I'm so fortunate that you care
about this old writer
I am no longer nervous about looking
into your eyes this day
Although I fear your gaze may
cause me to loose my way
I'd witness the changes to everything
down to your very soul
Protecting you and your heart
is to be my only goal
Please allow me on this day
to love you is all I ask of you
To take the bullets meant for
your heart and clear your view
Reciprocation not required but is
welcomed with open arms
To be the friend that you look to
for support and grounding charms
The one you call when your world goes sideways
A friend to help you pass through this phase

Catch Her If You Can

Catch her if you can
Escapes the limits of man
Lost her focus an' trips
Inner voice mutters slips
Notices pain in her hips
Eventually regains her grips
Don't count her out just yet
Or you'll be in her debt
Labour is never her short fall
Exercising is her morning call
Zeal comes naturally to her
Almost second nature as it were
Looks like major energy transfer

God Spent More Time On You

I'd like it if you were close to me
cuz it would mean the most to me
Heard bout the redness in your cheeks
as that tells me your heart is on fire
The gentleness of your whispered text
tells me you soul is full of desire
So if you open your heart and
allow me to slip on in
I promise to be gentle and
be the happiest I've ever bin
God spent more time on you

A Girl Like Mine

Get yourself a girl like mine
She be with me all the time
She's forever in my thought
She be the best I've got
She's my morning wake up call
And picks me up when I fall
And fall for her I did too
as into my heart, she flew
She has a dream in her eyes
and a smile on her face.
She sees things in me that I've
never seen, so much as a trace
She sends the heart eye
emoji after reading my poem
Amazing is how I feel now,
gone forever is the lonesome
I look forward to Sunday
evenings as I send her lines
Her Monday mornings are
for generating smiles and signs
Anything with a heart is
what I love to see best
And I look to the day she
rides the skys and comes west

Miss That Face

Sure going to miss that smiling face
and that amazing loving embrace
No poem can relay the sadness
your Canadian friends
feel with this madness
that keeps the brightest
shine from gracing our
little Kamloops town this July
We get it and know it's not a
easy choice.

We Will Meet Again

You've been gone these many many week
During which the world has gone, up the creek
Please know you are missed by us all
And we'll keep hoping you can visit by fall
The waterfalls, the mountains, and all the rivers
Will be here till winter and will cause you shivers
You are worth the wait because of your shine
We'll eventually meet at the gate of an airline
For now there will be messages and poetry
From your Canadian land to your home country
So please stay safe, stay heathy and take care
We will meet again, sometime, somehow, some where

Minutes

The single most valuable gift
you have at your disposal is time
You have been kind enough to share those
minutes that are so precious and prime
Those minutes cannot be bought
or stolen, only given away
And I so very thankful you chose to
share them with me on any given day
You are a true blessing with your
wonderful attitude and incredible shine
I always look forward to those minutes
when our schedules merge and align
I'm so appreciative of you sharing
your time and your story
Like everyone, it's had it's ups
and downs, it's dips and it's glory
So when you're down and lose
a wee bit of that beautiful shine
Remember that I've got your back
just like you have mine
If you flash up that smile and
let it brighten up your day
Then you'll breeze through
whatever barriers come your way

Bits an' Pieces

She's made of so many
wonderful bits and pieces
That my love and admiration
of her never ceases
The lack of filters gives
her a view so different
While everyone sees a raging
river she sees a caressing current
Sees the opponents on
the other side of the net
As friends, she just hasn't met yet.

She Makes Me Feel

I'm up every morning before the rooster
crows and before the sun breaks
I look forward to a day chasing
waterfalls, hiking, and checking out lakes
It's become a habit or maybe tradition
to send her a poem once a week
Hopefully the next we see each other
she won't mind a kiss on the cheek
She carries a majestic personality that has
my love, my respect, and my admiration
I've seen the effort and drive she puts into
building a strong and stable foundation
The future holds the last day of classes,
last 10k run, and an amazing graduation
I'm her biggest fan, so pleased to watch her
walk the walk of pride and affirmation
She makes the dreamer in me, keep on,
keeping on, dreaming strong
I can't help but keep dreaming
of her all day and all night long
She makes me want to write a song
about being loved and blessed
That song will speak to holding her close,
with her head on my chest
I now believe in who I thought I could be,
because of how she makes me feel
There's times that I find it hard to
believe that life she shares is real
She makes me realize how
fortunate I am, with what I own
I have my health, a roof, a table,
and best of all, her on my phone

Nothing But A Dream

Walked in with nothing
but guts and a dream
Left months later with
muscles busting the seam
Took those dreams and
weathered the storm
Hard work, daily 10k's,
have become the norm
She runs, she jumps,
she spikes, and she scores
Proud to say that I became an'
always will be a fan of yours

In Those Yoho Mountains

Somewhere in those Yoho mountains
is a natural bench of rock
We will stumble along and when we find it,
this is where we will sit and talk
Other than Instagram, it's been months
since I have seen your pretty face
However the thing I miss more
than anything is that loving embrace
I love the merging of energies
when our arms wrap around each other
It's all encompassing but the opposite
of feeling I'm about to smother
So I anxiously await that for that
feeling when next you fly west.
Although I believe you have enjoyed all,
which poems spoke to you best?
I ask her to look into her memories
and speak to the three that hit home
The ones that make her homesick
for places, friends, and where they roam
I tell this girl that I'm up
for anything you wanna do with me
I'll do anything that pleases
your soul and sets you free
Like a boomerang, a bounce, or a loop,
I'm looking for a do over an over
Those conversations that have you and I
making memories rolling in clover
So start your Monday morning
run with this little poem in your head
Or push it aside and simply
concentrate on beast mode instead
She makes the dreamer in me
keep dreaming strong
I keep dreaming of her
all day and all night long

Far From Where She Started

So far from where she started.
just look at her now
Lean and, shredded,
should be taking a bow
Where there is nothing
but the utmost respect
Every shift, every workout
till there is nothing left
She embodies the saying
'nothing left on the table'
Pushes through the back pain
with everything she's able
Her Canadian blood pushes her
to play through a broken leg
Sucks it up, finishes the game,
as she's too proud to beg
Every time I see her,
I immediately go to my favourite place
It's where her hugs feel their best
and put a smile on my face
I circle the date on my calendar,
wait these long lonely weeks
Knowing that I'll do my best
to satisfy whatever she seeks
Be that a walk along
a quiet mountain trail
Or riding the Pipe Mountain
Coaster down the rail
Feeling the fresh river
mist along with the July sun
So proud of her and the friendship begun

Stuck in My Head

I've got you stuck inside my head
Not sure if it's due to words you said
Or the dreams I have late at night
How your words seemed to fit just right
They were about dropping your guard
And how you were hurting real hard
You said you didn't want them to know
That your walls were built of snow
A warm heart can melt those walls
As they tumble when summer calls
This is intimacy, when the walls drop
Thoughts flow back and forth nonstop
Sharing those heartfelt thoughts
When you know it'll tie you in knots
Once broken, I now appreciate what's mine
And those in my circle, that truly shine
A gift from me to you that will forever be
Telling you that "You're safe with me"

Over Qualified

Rolls into town like a gentle winter storm
She's unique in her black police uniform
As different as that long mane she shakes free
Looks real pretty as she smiles at me
Nope, it's not me she's smiling at
Cute dude behind me but I'm ok with that
I still caught a glimpse of that beautiful smile
Nothing shines brighter than a smile with style
Her mere presence warms the soul
Stay safe and git yourself home whole
Thanks for coming and saving the day
Take that long road home, come what may
She be smart, she be strong, she be attractive
She be creative, be be caring, and she stays active
So why then, I ask, is that beautiful woman single?
Answer is real simple - she's simply over qualified

Fire in her eyes

She has a fire in her eyes
tears won't quell the flames
No matter how much she cries
Her shine is impossible to define
I have much love, for this friend of mine
Her many pieces and little bits
Some misses but most are hits
A smile and a tilt of her head
A handshake or an hug instead
She has a look and smile for a stranger
Without warning him of the danger
She could have told him of her powers
That will have them chatting for many hours
In all my many years, I've met very few
That carry a shine like the one around you
During these maddening events
Protect your shine, when danger presents

Be That Girl

In a world where you
can be anything, anytime
Be that girl, that one
with the amazing shine
She smiles that smile of hers
that's truly very unique
She shines from within then she
gives you that smile you seek
So all you want to do is hang
with her, never let go, never part
It's her soul that reaches out
and wraps around your heart
She carries magic through her
eyes right down into her soul
Then sprinkles that magic as if
ove and tenderness was the goal

Dancing In The Moonlight

Dancing in the moonlight
is a lifelong dream
You, different from all
others, are perfect it seems
To find that spot where
feet find sandy ground
Turn on your favourite song
hold you close, turn you round
Whisper sweet nothings,
an' subtle truths in your ears
Tell of your beauty, inside
and out, that'll bring tears
Those tears are actually mine
as she's the greatest of all time

Glass Castles

Where would you like to go so we can sit and talk
He follows her down the path and onto the dock
No where special she says with a enormous smile
Someplace quiet, where we can be alone for awhile
Off come the boots and dips her feet in the water
So warm she says, hope it don't get any hotter
She speaks softly of building glass castles
She knows all about planning and hassles
We all know that glass can be shattered
Leaving you broke, busted, and tattered
And while you sit quietly and dream
Keep in mind that but a single beam
Can be refracted into an array of colour
The reds, yellows, blues, and all the others
Like those broken ones that discharge a shine
Few can see the likes of yours is but a sign
Yours comes once you're sitting on the wharf
While you sip your morning coffee,
listening to the surf

The Scent Of Water

She loves the
sound and
scent of water.
The smell of an
incoming storm
triggers her senses,
sending it's energy
throughout her.

Thoughts When I Put'em To Pen

When I take my thoughts and put em to pen
Do you enjoy these stories of stars and women
Do I make you cry or do you smile real wide
How do they make you feel, deep inside?
Will you let me take you on a journey of your own
I'll look at your life and how much you've grown
I'll pen where you come from and what you've done
Where do you work, and what you do for fun
So tell me, What's in your heart
Where do I begin, where do I start
Who, Where, What do you love?
Do you look to the God above
I pick only the positive bits and pieces
If you're willing to share your
social media with it's releases
What's the best of Twenty Nineteen?
What's the happiest you've ever been
Or the saddest time you've gone thru
Are you alone or a couple of two?
Where in twenty twenty do you want to go
Are you looking for sunshine or powder snow
Going forward what is it that you dream
Knowing that reality can be a wee bit mean
Do you spend time healing old scars
Or wrenching on old bikes and cars
Could it be that your hobby is horses or dogs
Or do you pen as a writer of blogs
Speak to me of that one song
That one that makes you strong
And the one that makes you weak
So weak that your eyes leak

Hair Is BloodShot Red

Her hair is a bloodshot red
Falling loose as she stared straight ahead.
We talked about the illness we hate and dread.
Of childhood fears and dislikes that
pulled us into hugs and likes.
She hails out of Thompson Manitoba
Came early to BC to collect her diploma
A miner's work ethic she learned from her dad
A true pleasure to have her as a friend and comrade
Under all that hair, bone, and muscle
Is her 'lets get the job done' kinda hustle
Her flip side gets real quiet and real serious
And there's a smile showing a hint of mischevious
We're happy she came to live in Kamloops
We see her running through our hills with her hoops

A true friend is someone who
asks how you are and sticks around
to hear the answer
C.D.

Chapter Five

87 Paying Attention
88 Magnolia Smile
89 Whose Going To Love Her
90 My Heart, My Protection
90 Bonanza Ledge
91 She Said She'd Say Hi
92 Introduced Me To A Squat Rack
93 My Best Moments
94 The Book
95 Turn Loose My Gypsy Soul
96 No More Flowers
97 No Matter What
98 She Calls Him Hank
99 She's A Mustang Kinda Girl
100 Your Journal
101 She's A Dreamer
102 She Blushed
103 You Shine So Bright
104 It's About The Ride
105 I Can't Sing Or Dance
106 I Think I'll Stay
107 Heer Eyes
108 Take Note
109 To Be Seen
110 Whole Lot Special Woman

Paying Attention

How often do we miss the gift
of truly paying attention
This is a blessing definitely
worthy of a solid mention
Often we hear the song however
we miss that subtle riff
We grasp the package but miss
the meaning of the gift
So look for the one thing usually missed
The fleck of green in those brown eyes
Or the Duchene smile that began as a smirk
And the coffee creamer that's actually a perk
When we look to our friends do we see the Gemini
When we look at the forest do we miss the tree
See a real pretty woman but
we fail to notice the shine
Looking at our parents do we
see a smidgeon of time
When we have love to share
do we miss the love we receive
Do we tell stories and miss
the tales that our eyes believe
Maybe we fail to notice
she has some gangster under that crown
That our friend with depression
that's showing signs of feeling down

Magnolia Smile

She be brunette haired beautiful
with a Magnolia kinda smile
She is such a kind soul
I was intrigued and we chatted a while
Would have stayed all day
if given the choice but duty came
We talked of our dreams
making memories of same
Her eyes are gates to her
beautiful soul and highlight her smile
This is one of those smiles
that resonates for a good long while
Smiles and laughter comes
easily to this amazing woman
Intuition screams of a beautiful
personality and really kind human
She forever brightened up my day and
is the single reason I smiled today
Has a volleyball team to protect her
and they do whatever she say
I'll see her again one day out
chasing waterfalls and mountain hiking
Here's hoping she up for a bit of convo
as she's got personality I'm truly liking
So I ask this of you, show me the way,
give me direction while taking my hand
In the waterfalls mist,
and on the mountain top, together we will stand
Over the next few years
you will come and go across that open sea
You'll always be in my heart,
it's one place you will remain and always be

Whose Going To Love Her

Whose going to love her when she goes dark
When depression comes and grabs her heart
Who will remember her love of real cheese
Will you walk beside her as she defeats her disease
Are you willing to listen while she learns guitar
As she strums and misses that cord trying to be a star
When she sings along to a song Shinedown makes
And she sounds more like a Ford with bad brakes
You willing to walk the aisles filling the cart
Knowing that feeding that crew, this is but a start
Christmas is coming, so where's the turkey and tree
Time to step up, help out, and be all you can be
All these things that some would call negative
Those ways you prove your intentions are positive
She's really picky and truly is one of a kind
Bring your absolute best cuz she's the best you'll ever find

My Heart, My Protection

There's a pretty woman that I kinda recognize
I've seen her before but not with those eyes
She's been hurt and is still afraid
it'll happen again
She remembers the sleepless nights and the pain
I'm taking her on an adventure, making memories
She'll see a different world and write new stories
This world is hers and where she
is the one in control
No longer answering to another
and having to pay toll
She knows this is simply an act
of kindness without flair and styles
While the reality is expectations
are for laughter and smiles
You are safe with me and to you,
I offer respect and admiration
Caring for you means, I give you freely,
my heart, my protection

Bonanza Ledge

High up on Barkerville Mountain
is a place called Bonanza Ledge
A place where underground miner's
work with pick and sledge
It's Christmas time and it's gotten
real quiet around here
Kitchen is shut down so it's off to the
Jack O Clubs for liquid cheer
Rhea and Joseph come visit
as it got real lonely down below
Justin and Jay spend the night
hoping and praying it'll finally snow
Kayly straps on a sled and climbs
the mountain like she's at X-Games
Twisting and turning, yanking and
cranking all round these old claims
There's Brenda on her grader,
winging off the berm
And Matt's on OT once again,
taking Marcel!s turn
Tyler switched generators,
knocking out the lights for a minute
Rock truck backs in as the excavator
swings and puts muck in it
I've worked in the mines since
I snuck in the first one at seventeen
This one not so bad as it's only
dropping down to minus eighteen
Coal mines in that black dusty hole
that never allowed you to feel clean
Took an upgrade and went to Afton
for a year mining that copper green
Them boys and girls felt it was ripe
for a strike so I packed up once more
                              Cont'

Found myself signed up and grabbing
a new parka at the Cassiar store
Three years crawling in asbestos was enough
for me so it's Ontario I go
Coldest I'll ever have felt was on that
waste dump at fifty five below
Now a father of three it was time to
pack and move back to B.C.
Fifteen years at Endako learning
the fundamentals of a flotation machine
Nine Eleven seen me working at
Kemess on a four by three
Another fifteen year stint,
and then it's the dreaded pink slip for me
So as I sit on The Ledge and ponder
and recall how it was I got here
I think there's got to be a way
I could find my way to QR and disappear

She Said She'd Say Hi

She said she'd reach out sometime down the road
She may have gotten lost cuz she never showed
Or she took a road less travelled down memory lane
I remember her talking of her desire to fly a plane
Or perhaps she recalled the time on Ferguson dock
Where we walked, sat,
and found time to sit and talk
We moved up on the rise and
found a bench where we sat
We chatted about life, death,
dying and things like that
I wonder if she recalls that
we never talked about the weather
Everyone talks about the weather
but not us, we never ever
Our conversations revolved around
life and all about living
All those things that make life
full of asking and forgiving
Or like me she enjoyed that day
of photoshoot, hair, and makeup
Which spoke of friendship, trust,
living life, and getting done up
Don't recall ever seeing you shine
so bright as you did that day
You smiled, you laughed,
you enjoyed yourself,
everything was A-OK
I Remember well, the smiles and
laughter coming from us two
And how much more relaxed and
how much safer it felt for you
Recalling flowers that no longer
serve a purpose or a meaning
And that books lead to better thoughts
and have her dreaming
But I hope she'll always remember
her "no matter what" guy
No-one wants their last memory
to be of that friend saying "goodbye"

Introduced Me To a Squat Rack

I met her a while back when
she introduced me to a squat rack
I simply can't imagine starting
a friendship any better than that
I will share one little not so secret
fact that everyone knows
When this woman smiles
she absolutely radiates and glows
Her reaction when I told her
that my son had died was pure empathy
Never before nor since have
I experienced such unbridled sympathy
She literally reached into my soul
and absorbed some of my pains
Having her enter my life is simply
one of my life's biggest gains
I'll take her to a Tofino beach
so she can watch a slow moving satellite
After a day of learning to surf
and as the days turns into night
It's hard to tell if the stars in the sky
will outshine the stars in her eyes
She brings out the biggest of smiles
in me as I see her face in the skies
No-one hugs like this woman can,
her hug is an amazing sensation
Where her strength and her gentleness
are an perfect combination
Those hugs are my favourite of all time
and have become my addiction
She's my Miss Adventure and I love her
with a full on conviction

The Book

The Tuesday morning around came the mail man
Walking his route on Pearl Drive
with package in hand
Could never of known what an amazing
text he delivers
The book he carries would give
the woman inside icy shivers
This book tells the story of her
previous life and her pain
Stories of mental abuse such as being
called bipolar and insane
This manuscript carries sad truths
and describes pure evil
Bound to cause release as well
as bring calm to previous upheaval
The word contained herein will
describe pains not often known
As well as how to find overdue healing,
rebirth, and a life reborn
A narcissist's handbook on how
to destroy a gentle human
In detail how to slowly grasp
a kind soul and make it worsen
It also shows a victim that she
was targeted and set up
And the only way to save herself
is to call it quits and break up
Leave this sorry SOB that pretends
to be kind and generous
When all it did was spew lies and venomous

Turn Loose My Gypsy Soul

It's time to turn loose my Gypsy Soul
Ninety Seven is waiting, so let's roll
Dance through those corners and dips
Been a long winter, I'm needing these trips
Road has spots that'll make your hair curl
But out there a ways, is a real pretty girl
She smiles then flashes her baby blues
A keeper by any standards, that I'd chose
A Whiskey Girl is what Toby sings of her
Beer drinking, muscle car kind, if it were
Me, I kinda like the shape of her legs
As she settles over an' finds those rear peg

No More Flowers

You realize, saying no more flowers
Is akin to stealing superman's powers
Or pulling the mask off the Lone Ranger
It's simply fraught with stranger danger
You know you'll have your down days
If can't send daisies, I'll need other ways
Maybe a cab delivery of a certain kinda tea
An XL, two chia bags, and a half of honey
Dead people get flowers and you're still alive
How do I solve the conundrum, when I arrive
I got it - Oh yes I believe I do!!!
A poem about flowers is what I'll spew
So here it is. On top of the roses
Sat the daisies in special poses
Wrapped an XL coffee with two milk
Careful now so you don't spill on that gown of silk
Try as she might she sees flowers in her mind
Knowing that tricky bastard got her this time
Her shine bounces back as she's all aglow
Happy he hung around cuz he's good to know

No Matter What

There's a girl! A real pretty girl
but that's not why she's unique
It's her soul and what shines from
within when she gives you a peek
She lives a long way from me
kinda like over yonder and back east
I don't get to see her as often
as I'd like so I'm acting the Beast
But she's with me whenever I write
As is the case as I scribe this night
When I'm in camp for a 14 day post
Is when I miss her shine the most
I love you girl but don't worry yourself bout that
Cuz it's not the kind with butterflies in the gut
It is the kind that truly never comes to an end
Put me on that list called 'no matter what' friend
I told her it's platonic,
I'm doing my best and I'm ok with that
How do I explain that I would love
to be her "no matter what"
Someone she can call 'no matter what'
if it's huge or microscopic
Someone she can vent at 'no matter what'
regardless of the topic
Someone that she doesn't need to explain
herself to 'no matter what'
So please keep me in mind and
I promise to be here, no if, and, or but

A Mustang Kinda Girl

She's a Mustang kinda girl
taking on the world by herself
She loves the day that allows her to take
the car keys off the shelf
She's every man's dream being beautiful,
blue eyed, with hair the colour of cream.
A play outside kinda girl, that'll jumps on a sled
or a quad and take it for a whirl
This is the one girl you hang onto
and dare not let slip away
Pray you'll look deep into those baby blues
every given Sunday
I look to that day so that I may
speak directly to her soul
To speak of her gentleness while
willing to pay any toll

Your Journal

I know a woman, she's a real
pretty northern girl
With beautiful black hair
that has a hint of curl
Somewhere she lost her
identity and her worth
Needs to re-examine her
ties to the moon and earth
Your journal, you just might
change the world with that
Let it speak to your love of baseball
and your times at bat
Right when you are in the middle
of the storm, break the rules
Write to the dreams and the nightmares
of our political fools
Write to love of your children
and their children
And to the breaking of the chains
of memories hidden
You have it in you to move folks
with your stories and yarns
How Shadowman reaches for you
with his whisky and charms
I will be here to remind you
of your mountaintop dream
With the bad days behind you
and never again to be seen
A single long breath out as you feel
yourself slide forward
That wing suit slicing through the air
like King Arthur's sword.

She's A Dreamer

Like John Lennon she too is a dreamer
Dreams of ocean beaches and a long hot summer
Awakens to the day and unsure of her choices
Does she listen to the whispers
or sing with the voices
You will never see yourself the same way
After you see what I've seen today
You too will wonder how you missed this love
That encases you like a soft leather glove
I seen a side of her that she rarely shows
When she allows me in where no-one goes
It's where that shine begins from a single spark
Like a flint striking carbon steel in the dark
That spark begins to glow and slowly grows
Like a bulb that spreads into a beautiful rose
That single rose spreads into a full on bouquet
She steps out of the darkness and takes on the day

She Blushed

It's a good thing this turning
red and beginning to blush
Science says it's the opening of
your capillaries and feeling the rush
Science also says it's an indication
that you are feeling an attraction
I have every intention of seeing
you turn that special shade of red
You are different which is
attractive when all is done and said
I suspect it has been a long
while since anyone spoke to your soul
This I say to you, you are safe
with me and will have total control
I reminded of Toby Kieth's Whiskey
Girl whose got a 69 Mustang
Four on the floor and you oughta
hear them pipes ring
So sit back, bring Toby's
Whiskey Girl up on the net
Then tell me a story bout
how strong your feelings get

You Shine So Bright

You shine so bright that
those with evil in their heart
will fear your approach.
Hardest part of being an Empath
is feeling someone lie to you.
It is the one thing that truly
breaks your heart and makes you
question - WHY WHY WHY
Your personality is so infectious
folks just want to hang with you

It's About The Ride

Everyone has heard the one about
"it's not about the destination"
It's about the ride and the wind
in your face sensation
And as the miles slide by
you can feel them filling your soul
With that single headlight cutting
through a night as black as coal
Push too hard into those corners
and it begins to slide
If I'm writing this I'm ok
but this time maybe I died
For my epitaph 'he was reborn
and he truly lived his life'
Used his time wisely till it
was severed like a knife

Can't Sing or Dance

You don't know this but I
can't sing nor can I dance
However what I'd love
to do is hold your hand's
To feel the energies
flow from you to I
As I don't want to
let this chance go by
I'll take the few bits an'
pieces you send my way
A wee little bit of love
that'll surely make my day
A piece of your heart has
pulled me in from the start
That hug of yours is
second to none
Allowing me to believe
that I'm "The One"

I Think I'll Stay

Every night I have
the strangest feeling
It's all those stitches
and scars that are healing
Long ago heartbroken,
my blood flowed like a river
And the love you shared that
I thought would last forever
The day you came into
my life I felt blessed
All the days I've lived
that one was the best
Now is not the time to
let go and walk away
But I deserve more than
half a heart so I think I'll stay

Her Eyes

She uses her eyes
to speak the words
her soul is saying.
She sends kisses with
but a subtle look.
Through her eyes
she opens her soul
and allows you
to see inside
when you look into
the depths of her
eyes seeking her soul
but instead you
find yourself lost

Take Note

Take note
that what
you offer
can be the
light that
shines into
someone's soul

To Be Seen

She doesn't
shine to be seen,
She shines
because that's
who she is

Whole Lot Of Special Woman

If she talks to the universe about how to care for you and deals in the spiritual world on your behalf, That's a whole lota special woman!

Chapter Six - Shorts

110 Wednesday Evening

111 Trust Is A Terrible Thing To Lose

112 Count Stars And Satellites

113 Some Call Her Mustang

114 Favourite Flower

115 Less Than 100%

116 How Did You Love

117 What You Mean

118 Your Thoughts

119 Tough Times

120 Different

121 Paths Cross Once Again

122 It's 3AM

123 I've Always Known

124 Be Her

125 Offers

126 Threw Them All Away

127 As They Pass

128 Without A Tether

129 Homebase

130 Simple Question Really

Wednesday Evening

This woman can
take a Wednesday
evening and with a
come hither smile
turn it into a Friday
night party for two.

Trust Is A Terrible Thing to Lose

Once again I read your Shadowman story
with its sadness and feeling down
No signs of happiness or of smiles
but plenty of misery and frown
You needed a friend when I let you down
you needed someone to hold your hand
Trust! It's a terrible thing to loose
But does not begin to compare to abuse

Count Stars And Satellites

I'd like to come count stars
and satellites with you
On a warm summer nights
laying by the sea with that
beautiful woman next to me
I'd like you to look deep into my soul
You may wanna hide once when
you see what's taken toll

Some Call Her Mustang

Some call her Mustang
Others call her Whiskey
Jill is the name she gave up to me
She just may be the one, holding the key
I'll use all six gears going to see her today
Twist hard on the right, and come what may
It's great to feel the knees in the breeze
It's better yet to put my arms round her
and feel her squeeze

Favorite Flower

What's her favorite flower
and is it window or aisle for her
Does she want to drive or is she
good with a sexy chauffeur
Metal music is her preference
and will be her goto tunes
Boots are for trails and
barefoot for sunny afternoons

Less Than 100%

I gave my word and unlike some,
I believe in loyalty and integrity
Again unlike some, I would never
trade either for ego or popularity
I do however refuse to be kept
around as an optional choice
I don't do less than a hundred percent
so long as I have a voice

How Did You Love

How did
you love?
What do
you leave
behind?

What You Mean To Me

If you only knew what
you mean to me
In a world where
my circle is kept small
It's not for you
to worry on, not at all

Your Thoughts

Your thoughts and the rest
Give me some of your best
Not always about a pretty face
It's bout the monsters you chase
Or the death of a loved son
And the adoption of a loved one
Sometimes about things you write
Or relationships that aren't real tight

Tough Times

She says tough times don't last
Tough people do as her goals are past
She sets a strong marker
against she'll be gauged
She is a warrior fighting
a personal war staged

Different

You know you're different
when you are a loner
by nature and feel isolated
While failing to fit
into today's standards
of careers, materialism,
and social status
to the point of being
referred to as offbeat,
unconventional,
and strange.

Paths Cross Once Again

It's amazing after these last couple
years our paths once again do cross
Call it destiny or call it meant to be,
whatever it is, it's just about us
It's not just about the
adventures we will experience
But the conversations
and the exploring of the curious

3AM

It's 3AM with
thoughts running wild
Memories of younger
days as a child
And about that
dream I'm chasing
Or that woman
that I love embracing
She hugs real tight
while passing energy
From her very soul to
fill the emptiness in me

I've Always Known

I've always
known one day
I'd lose you
not to some
handsome player
But to the
beautiful you
that's hidden
under all your
many layers

Be Her

In a world where you
can be anything, be Her
She is gorgeous and when
she smiles that smile of her's,
it captures your heart!
Her soul is so powerful,
when you look into her eyes,
they draw you in and
have you believing in love.

Offers

Many offers from those
that look to her beauty
None inquire as to
her hopes and dreams
They know not of her
wonderous heart nor
her beautiful soul
To look into her eyes is
to find yourself drowning
in a sea of delight

Couldn't Decide

She couldn't
decide who
to keep and
who to let go.
So she threw
them all away

Lost Her

Thought I lost
her but
she was never
really there

As They Pass

Some things look best
as they pass on through
However that certainly
doesn't apply to you
I like nothing better than
watching you shed your layers
Not to answer my wishes
but to answer your prayers

Without A Tether

I like you this
way without a tether
To your broken bits
and broken pieces
As I can put
them back together
And watch the
way your
shine increases

Homebase

Whenever you wander
and disappear
Remember your home
base is always here
As he points and taps
twice above his heart
For our friendship will
never fail nor fall apart

A Simple Question

A simple question really
When I feel my best
Who do I hang with
Whose head on my chest?

A true friend is someone
who asks how you are and sticks around
to hear the answer
C.D.

Made in the USA
Middletown, DE
09 March 2021